Inspire Your Power

AN INSPIRATIONAL JOURNAL OF LOVE
AND JOY FOR KIDS WITH DYSLEXIA

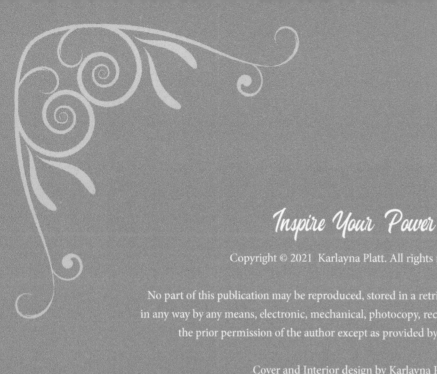

Inspire Your Power

Cover and Interior design by Karlayna Platt
Published in the United States of America
Hardback ISBN: 978-163760579-0

EDU026020 | EDUCATION / Special Education / Learning Disabilities
Education (Facts about Dyslexia)
Self Help (encouragement and tips)
Psychology (empowerment and motivational)

First Edition

25 24 23 22 21 20 / 10 9 8 7 6 5 4 3 2 1

ABOUT
the Author

Karlayna Platt is a sophomore at Westlake Academy. As a young girl, Karlayna was diagnosed with dyslexia and has worked tirelessly to ensure her diagnosis did not slow her down academically, socially or emotionally. With a strong passion for helping others, she decided to create a book with the purpose of inspiring children with her gift of tenacity, growth and determination. Karlayna has a bright future, exemplifying a balanced profile. She enjoys playing on her high school volleyball team and contributing to her community through National Charity League, all while demonstrating strong academic success within an International Baccalaureate School. Karlayna attributes her accomplishments to strong intervention at an early age and the support of her dedicated family along with her personal drive for achievement. Her personal philosophy revolves around the idea that every individual is capable of overcoming challenges. She hopes children of all ages will look inside themselves for success and discover their own POWER.

Keep an eye out for the
HIDDEN LETTERS
(9) K's, (9) M's and (9) P's
as this is one of my family traditions that spans multiple generations!

THIS JOURNAL IS CREATED FOR YOU TO REFLECT, GROW AND INSPIRE YOUR POWER.

FROM THE AUTHOR:

Inside this book, you will find inspiration in the form of empowering quotes, letter tracing, coloring, fun facts about dyslexia, as well as tips and quotes that I have found helpful during my journey. Many children with dyslexia are creative with intuitive abilities of pattern recognition and strong spatial knowledge. We are known to be creative and demonstrate the skills of an open-minded thinker. Personally, I discovered this to be true as I found myself excited and empowered by the digital design process while creating this book.

ENJOY!

FUN FACTS

Children with dyslexia are creative and have a high level of intelligence.
Brilliant minds with dyslexia include: Albert Einstein, Alexander Graham Bell, Thomas Edison, Winston Churchill, Benjamin Franklin, and Wolfgang Amadeus Mozart.

Children have a 50% chance of having dyslexia if one parent exhibits the trait & a 100% chance if both parents have dyslexia.

Children with dyslexia do not typically read words backwards. The "b-d" letter reversal is caused by difficulty in interpreting left and right.

DYSLEXIA IS MY SUPER POWER!

Orginal Photo by Karlayna Platt

Get creative and color!

Let your light...

HOW DO YOU SHINE?

SHINE
SHINE
SHINE

WRITE WITH ME!

Trace the phrases below for some writing practice!

You are smarter than you think!

You are smarter than you think!

You are smarter than you think!

WHAT ARE YOUR GIFTS?

EVERY CHILD IS GIFTED, THEY JUST UNWRAP THEIR PACKAGES AT DIFFERENT TIMES.

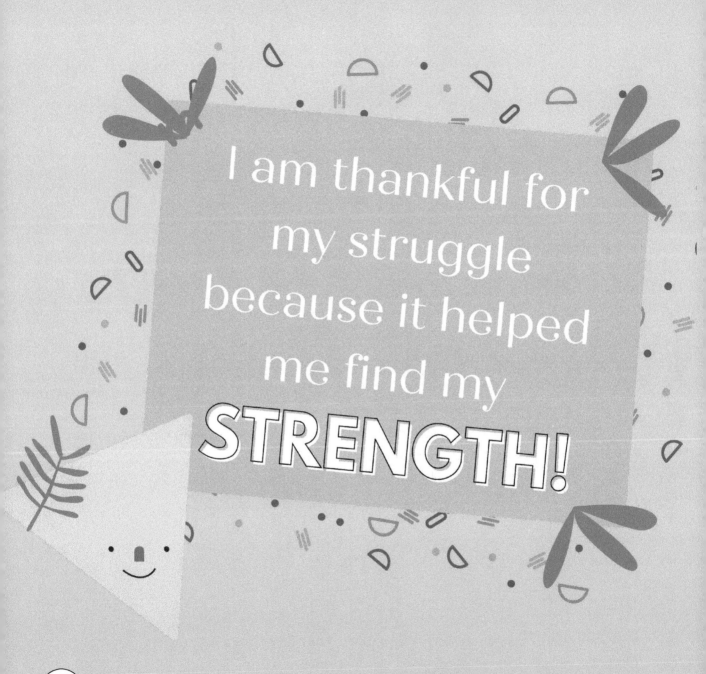

I am thankful for my struggle because it helped me find my STRENGTH!

FUN FACTS

Famous People with Dyslexia
Walt Disney
Tom Cruise
Steve Jobs
Jennifer Aniston
Patrick Dempsey
Cher
Steven Spielberg

People with dyslexia have a difficult time learning to associate letters with sounds. As early readers, they struggle to read basic words such as: "that", "the" and "in".

It is no use going back to yesterday, because I was a

DIFFERENT

person then.

— Lewis Carroll

WRITE WITH ME!

Trace the phrases below for some writing practice!

Take chances, make mistakes, that's how you grow.

Take chances, make mistakes, that's how you grow.

Take chances, make mistakes, that's how you grow.

Your Journey

is like no other.

Your talent

is unique to you.

Your gifts

can make a difference.

Get creative and color!

WRITE WITH ME!

Trace the phrases below for some writing practice!

Follow your dreams!

Follow your dreams!

Follow your dreams!

14

How can the sky be the limit when there are footprints on the moon?

WHAT ARE YOUR GOALS?

15

IT DOESN'T MATTER HOW SLOW YOU GO AS LONG AS YOU DON'T STOP

Get creative and color!

What keeps you going?

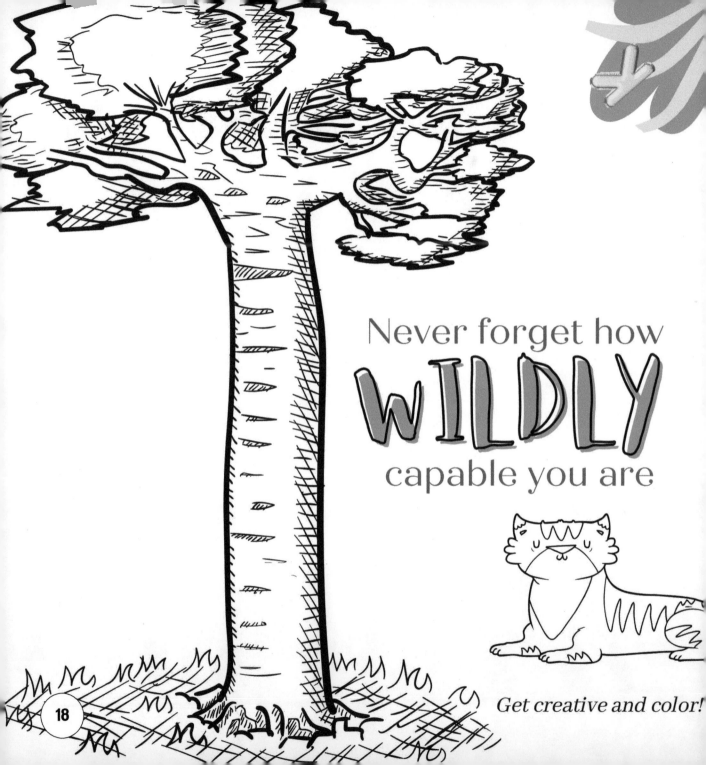

Never forget how **WILDLY** capable you are

Get creative and color!

Get creative and color!

FUN FACTS

It is estimated that 1 in 5 children have dyslexia. Dyslexia effects girls and boys equally.

25-40% of children with dyslexia also have ADHD.

Children with dyslexia score higher on a test when they have the test read out loud and are given more time for completion. Complicated directions and long lists can seem overwhelming and difficult for these children.

Stop doubting yourself!
You are so strong,
show the world what
you've got!

WHAT MAKES YOU STRONG?

EVERY FLOWER IS UNIQUE

Orginal Photo by Karlayna Platt

Get creative and color!

What makes you unique?

EVERYTHING WHALE BE ALRIGHT!

Get creative and color!

FUN FACTS

Dyslexia does not
discriminate.
It affects ethnic
and socioeconomic
backgrounds equally.

BE
BRAVE
BE
STRONG
BE
YOU!

26

FUN FACTS

Children with dyslexia tend to have common characteristics. However, each individual is unique and symptoms can range from mild to severe.

People with dyslexia best use the right side of their brain, which is associated with art, emotion, spatial relationships, intuition and synthesizing of ideas.

Children affected have trouble remembering dates, names, telephone numbers and random lists.
Learning a foreign language is often a challenge.

Believe that you
are far
BIGGER
than Dyslexia

WRITE WITH ME!

WRITE WITH ME!

Trace the phrases below for some writing practice!

A hero lies in you.

A hero lies in you.

A hero lies in you.

29

Go Out on a Limb.... that is where the Fruit is!

-Frank Scully

FUN FACTS

Common Skills

- Good at solving puzzles
- Strong spatial awareness
- Excellent thinking skills
- Display strong imagination
- See the big picture

Signs of Dyslexia

- Learn new words slowly
- Struggle with spelling
- Avoid reading
- Difficulty summarizing stories
- Problem with memorizing
- Trouble with math problems and foreign languages

WRITE WITH ME!

Trace the phrases below for some writing practice!

Think positive thoughts

Think positive thoughts

Think positive thoughts

32

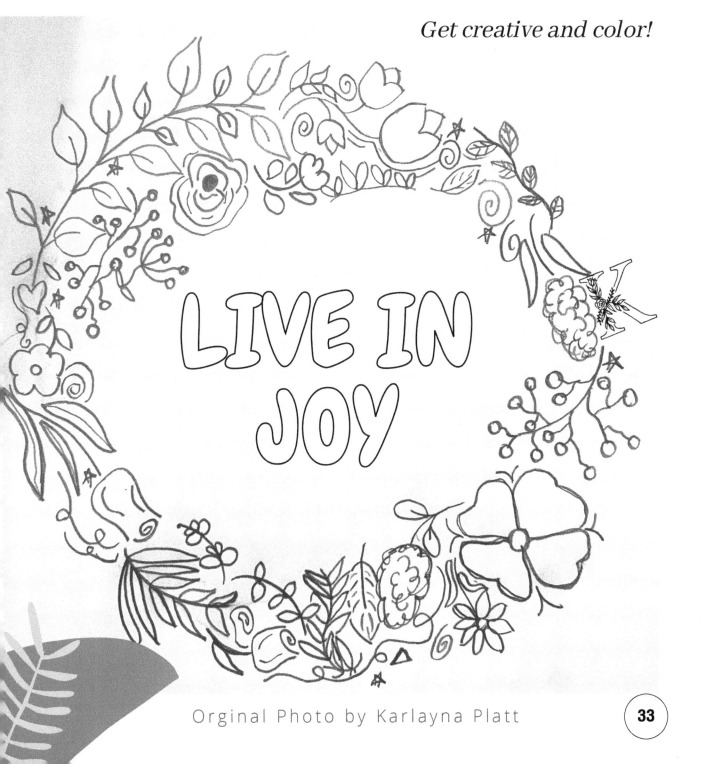

Orginal Photo by Karlayna Platt

BELIEVE

in yourself and all that you are, and

KNOW

that there is something inside you

that is

GREATER

than any

OBSTACLE

Write your thoughts:

WHAT SETS YOU APART MAKES YOU GREAT

WRITE WITH ME!

Trace the phrases below for some writing practice!

You are capable of amazing things.

You are capable of amazing things.

You are capable of amazing things.

What are your favorite things to do?

WHEN EVERYTHING FEELS LIKE
AN UPHILL STRUGGLE,
JUST THINK OF THE VIEW FROM THE TOP

Orginal Photo by Karlayna Pla

WRITE WITH ME!

Trace the phrases below for some writing practice!

Keep Moving Forward.

Keep Moving Forward.

Keep Moving Forward.

Get creative and colo

you are one
in a melon!

Don't settle for one scoop!

M♡

WRITE WITH ME!

Trace the phrases below for some writing practice!

Impossible is just an
opinion.

Impossible is just an
opinion.

Impossible is just an
opinion.

45

what is your favorite color?

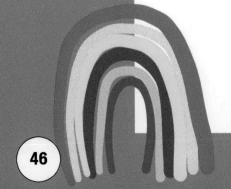
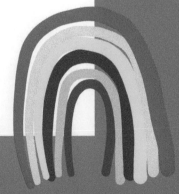

YOU ARE A RAINBOW OF POSSIBILITY

I am not afraid o[f]
storms...
...for I am learning
how to
SAIL MY SHIP

WAYS TO SAIL YOUR SHIP

PERSONALLY, I FOUND THAT THE FOLLOWING STRATEGIES ARE EFFECTIVE IN MY DAILY LIFE:

- - - - - - - - - - - -

-MANAGE TIME WISELY

-EXERCISE AND STAY HYDRATED

-GET 8-10 HOURS OF SLEEP NIGHTLY

-DO SOMETHING CREATIVE

-BREAK UP LARGE PROJECTS INTO SMALLER TASKS

-TAKE DEEP BREATHS AND RELAX

-READ ALONG WITH AUDITORY BOOKS

-CELEBRATE ACCOMPLISHMENTS

REFERENCES

articles

Angela. "50 Interesting Facts About Dyslexia"
https://athome.readinghorizons.com/blog/50-interesting-facts-about-dyslexia

Dosomething.org. "11 Facts About Dyslexia" https://www.dosomething.org/us/facts/11-facts-about-dyslexia

The Understood Team. "What is Dyslexia"
https://www.understood.org/en/learning-thinking-differences/child-learning-disabilities/dyslexia/what-is-dyslexia

The Understood Team. "Types of Dyslexia: What Researchers Are Studying and Why"
https://www.understood.org/en/learning-thinking-differences/child-learning-disabilities/dyslexia/different-types-of-dyslexia

books

Whatever You Are, Be a Good One By Lisa Congdon

Wonderful You! By Carin Rockind

Made Out Of Stars By Meera Lee Patel

Believe By Dan Zandra and Kobi Yamada, designed by Jessica Phoenix and Vanessa Tippmann

CPSIA information can be obtained
at www.ICGtesting.com
Printed in the USA
LVHW071524130421
684378LV00011B/391

9 781637 605790